CIRCLE MEADOW

For Ma —
Who inspired
so many of these
poems and who
took such good
care of us in Fresno.

Love: Gerry
5 Aug. 74

CIRCLE MEADOW

Gerald Hausman

❖

THE BOOKSTORE PRESS
Lenox, Massachusetts

Copyright © 1972 Gerald Hausman
Library of Congress Catalog Card No. 72-75950
ISBN No. 0-912846-00-3
Illustrations by Bob Totten
Cover design by Sheila Granda
Printed by The Studley Press, Inc.

This book is for Lorry

CONTENTS

The Skin Walker

Part 1

The Skin Walker	15
In The Shade, Hiding	16
Santo Domingo	17
Rattlesnake Hunters	18
On The King's River	19
Ravens	21
Winter Dying, Cherry Hill Farm	22
Bounding Deer During The Eclipse Of The Moon	23
Sleeping Out	24

Part 2

Moonface	27
Walk Home, Sad	28
Thoughts Before Entering A Sauna Dream	29
After The Grand Illusion	30
For The Person Sitting In Darkness	31
Listening To Water On A Delivery Of Candles	32
For Bruce With The Black Book	33
Varaz	34
Poem For Lorry	35
Night Visit To The Summer House In Winter	36

CONTENTS cont.

CIRCLE MEADOW

Three Poems For My Father

November Sunday Rainy Day Dream	42
The Beaded Moccasins	43
Sid	44

Two Poems For My Mother

Dorothy Emma Little	46
Cleaning Out The Attic	47

Two Poems For My Brother

My Brother & Me	50
The Attic	53

Three Poems For Tommy

Tommy	56
Uncle Charlie	57
The Girl In The Woods/Flashback Nineteen Fifty-Eight	59

Six Poems For Myself

The Rubber Tree That Lived Twenty Winters	62
The Snake Nest Under The Willow Tree	63
The Cure	64
The Hired Hand's Cornfield Gift	65
The Days Of Yesteryear	66
My Brother & The Bull	67

ACKNOWLEDGEMENTS

Some of these poems originally appeared
in SAGE, DESERT REVIEW, and ARARAT.

THE
SKIN WALKER
Poems: 1969-70

✽

Part 1

The idea for the title of this section of poems was given to me by a Navajo friend when I lived in New Mexico. He was the first person to tell me about the magic powers of the feared secret members of the tribe, The Skin Walkers or Wolfmen. But it was several years after I left the west that I began to write these poems, which actually have little to do with the Indians, but everything to do with the poet, who wears the poem as if it were a wolf skin and travels in darkness looking for his own tracks amongst the others.

THE SKIN WALKER

Out of the brittle shell, by starlight
wolf fur on pale skin

The scents come back
soft hands leave hard paw treads

By dawn, the frayed magic
stuffed in a hollow tree

The scary daylight reminds us
we are all   He Who Walks
              In Skins

naked alone
furred in packs

IN THE SHADE, HIDING

I am hidden in a mesquite thicket
watching a gauze caterpillar's tent
soak up wind.

Black dog in spring snow-gully
makes pant rhythm
equal to sun, pine, stone.

I see myself in his heavy
bear's skin, caught by cold
sand, smelling roots, chewing
prickly pear—only the pink
tongue moves between the leaves.

SANTO DOMINGO

My boots stir up
yellow feathers of dust,
sun fire on every stone.

A child playing
sees us coming and cries.
Fat moccasined mother
chases after her,
turquoise squash blossom
bangs at her breast.

The child swooped up
from the white invaders.
I feel eyes of things
sparkle back
from sky-roof antlers,
the child's corn husk doll
eyeless, grinning in the dust.

RATTLESNAKE HUNTERS

Four stand with rifles, waiting
then sure whip-crack flash
pale smoke carried down mountain.

One long brown-scaled coil
becomes two
out of the dead writhing
the live diamond head
sprung, coiled, sprang again.

Both killed before sundown
I carried the one four-footer
heavy, headless weight
slung round my arm.

Once skinned, tiny gelatin eggs
slimed out her stomach
she made a fine belt
dark phase of summer timber rattler
around my waist.

ON THE KING'S RIVER

We swim in green cobbled
trout current
fins of river slime
cling to elbow and arm.

I here again Veron's Armenian
contempt for animals:
the seals off point sur
she said, were jivuhkh, dekheq
(slippery-homely)
and here I am—
mud puppy water lizard
basking in swamp silt shallows
of king's river backwash.

RAVENS

Four sea coast ravens
    on forest moss
        down-hooked beaks
    heavy feathers on head:
    green and purple in sun.
Suddenly they rise up
        two at a time
            jam down their starters
    roar off over junk-strewn tides,
    bright chrome and flame-black skin.
Then all we saw was their eyes,
        their hateful eyes
            were sunken in.

WINTER DYING, CHERRY HILL FARM

Last month
three feet off the ground
on hard snow

Where I walked
chill sunny air

My tracks gone down hill
snow and mud trickle

I am no longer walking
in the sky. Hidden warbler
overhead is a liar; prickles
in my leg from sitting down
too long.

Crows sing me on home
no poem
no spring
no flowers

BOUNDING DEER DURING THE ECLIPSE OF THE SUN

They stopped chewing bark
hollow night iris
saw the yellow sickle
vanish

Black sun
sent them bounding out
day moon light

Long medieval hounds
falcon-eyed
badger-toed
shred the red meat juice;
bright wine
of a maple sapling
ripped clean

SLEEPING OUT

Drunk in a cow meadow
I lay face up, early starshine.
Cows came out of the pine trees
one at a time to stare—
great liquid slow blink eyes,
milkweed breath.
A bold one thrust tongue
to my chin, backed up, puzzled.
Slowly they turned around
tails swishing, and ambled off
tired of flies, false salt blocks
too many milkings.
I stayed and watched, almost drowsing
until the last white of them
went out in the dark.

Part 2

MOONFACE

He has come for me again,
knocking on each of the twelve
windows of the house.

I cannot go with you—
I've wandered
these bent ridges
in lost bear madness
before.

My wife sleeps calmly
face to the window:
lone priestess who tans
in the moon.

WALK HOME, SAD

May stars
and the moon slides up the sky.
An old snake died in my dreams
last night: now, walking absently,
swollen roots
slither and hiss under my feet:
the night air steams
with the breath of asps.

THOUGHTS BEFORE ENTERING A SAUNA DREAM

Dry fire in the nostrils
the mind floats away
dragon-kite tussles wind eddies
blood roses on a trellis
rain water fall

Sinking deeper into summer
ice pours out of pores
grey rocks whistle
like marmots
sputter when sweat hits

I am dreaming now in the moss
waste furrows of a hundred
year old sleeping Kraken

AFTER THE GRAND ILLUSION

My fern has grown half-way
        up the mirror
chainsaw open-spaced teeth:
        diet of the stegosaurus,
other prehistoric plant eaters.

But I am a classic Meat Eater
        lover of boiled
steam-faced pig's head
        with laughing teeth.

FOR THE PERSON SITTING
IN DARKNESS

Your eyes grown blacker
by the minute
focus on the fur sinews
of egyptian cats,
hooded basilisks
dying out
green ages of plankton.

Behind your head, in the rain,
birds fly north into the trees.

LISTENING TO WATER ON A DELIVERY OF CANDLES

Frog babies
bleat in the pond.
I wish I could take off my skin
and swim into their black song.

FOR BRUCE WITH THE BLACK BOOK

Whatever the fire said
he heard and we missed,
for he was soon gone
to his room
and we could hear
his footfalls
up in the unquiet mad parapet
harassing the devils;
flailing their asses
with homemade spontaneous torches
of cactus pitch and lizard drool.

VARAZ

Varaz stood on the copper rib cage
of his flared-nostril metal horse,
blow torch on
in tropic valley heat.
His studio, a weedlot cubistic maze,
sun-peeled plaster and steel
sculptures rotting
in burning daylight.
We broke watermelon with him
and ate while the giant horse shimmered,
swam in the gold water
over our heads:
skulls rung hollow
blazed by sun fantasy.

POEM FOR LORRY

At the bottom of the twisted
stairs, under fern and blackberry
bushes, I sat in pine shade
on a bark-stripped log
and scribbled poems.
Yesterday I heard light steps
on the stairs above, branches
moved behind me. I'm writing,
I said without turning around.
She left quickly but I felt
her absence in the poem.
The notebook shut, I climbed
to the house. She was on the bed
crying.

NIGHT VISIT TO THE SUMMER HOUSE IN WINTER

The dark house, snow dusted,
a thousand summer fires
burnt out in the stones
of that fireplace.
The first thaw, february grass
chopped open for your grave,
and I was unable to say
what I felt to the black-clothes
people who prayed and wept.
But tonight, I can talk
in winter light, alone,
if you are around these summer woods:
the owls across the lake hoot coldly,
the ice-flow moves whitely
in frozen water.

CIRCLE MEADOW
Poems: 1970-71

*The poems circling backwards
in time, beginning with my
father's death and ending
with my first remembrance
of Cedar Run Farm—sometimes
I see our whole family,
living and dead, gather
full circle in a white meadow.*

Three Poems For My Father

NOVEMBER SUNDAY RAINY DAY DREAM

A fire to burn away
the bad angels.

        Steady hiss & purr

Dog sleeps by table
        dream-quiver paws
My wife on her side
of Navajo design

I keep trying to read, words blur.
Miles from any split-maple fire
      gloved plastic hands
          of no concern
touch a grey face man
who, in white hospital sleep
forgets that he is my father.

THE BEADED MOCCASINS

My father, before he died, whispered:
    "You must learn to relax"
faint smile.

His hospital roomate, fat Kraut
bellowing behind yellow curtain:
    "Hey, Hausman
    I got the octupusses
    they got hold my STAHMICK!"
My father (to me) :
    "He's like a headache,
    you get used to it."

All his life there was no headache
to compare with this bright-walled misery;
just when he got used to it, he died.

We picked up his belongings
at the undertakers—
    one adhesive taped alarm clock
    one twenty-year-old faded purple smoking jacket
    one old brown glass case & reading glasses
one pair beaded Cree Indian moccasins
hand-sewn by my brother
worn by my father
on his final painful
journeys from bed to bathroom.

SID

The man with the moustache
smiles, great swamp sunny weeds
one year ago, alive.

I refused his gifts
while he died slowly
big pine at the window
lightless green rime bedroom,
later I pocketed two pearl-handled knives
which I'd coveted since childhood,
nothing else.

I helped him shave one day
when hands were too weak
he used old bottle bay rum aftershave
sank back in bed.

"Even with a fool, something rubs off,"
he said, explaining his life.

It all rubbed off, memory & dream
and this photograph on my wall
of him smiling in the great swamp
stuck in the good & the bad weeds
a part, solidly apart.

Two Poems For My Mother

DOROTHY EMMA LITTLE

Something out of Wuthering Heights
Miss Havisham, perhaps

My mother's black towels over curtained windows
        kitchen chairs
           interlocked upside-down
        to halt the Cellar Monster

A fire in hot summer for the sparkle
A stove door held up by a stick
A freakish coon-cat for a pet

Her only safetly was my father
who poked in the dark with a flashlight
when the bedsprings
spoke to her one night

CLEANING OUT THE ATTIC

Down stairs
come the dinosaurs
asleep under attic dust
twenty years

"Oh, don't throw out the dinosaurs!
Children love them, they study them in school!"

Down come the crumpled giants
      (carried to Columbia School
      in a 36 Buick rumble seat
      my mother drove
      we yelled at stunned pedestrians & cops
      while brown-scarred allosaurus
      munched on head
      of three-horned triceratops)

"I can't give up my dinosaurs!"
shaking her head at the awesome vision
of an END, a millenial ice age
her life somehow stacked broken papery
on livingroom dusty floor

"There'll never be dinosaurs
like them again,
just *look* at those CLAWS!"

Two Poems For My Brother

MY BROTHER AND ME

Kitchen knife aimed at the bookcase
        you were on the telephone
           talking to your girl, ducked quick
             MISSED
Then there was the ovenblast
        blew off your beard
terrible howling in the tumbleweeds
           me running out
           shouting:
"I didn't leave the gas on,
I didn't . . ."
A few months later I kicked over
        a boulder
        halfway up a mesa by moonlight
buckskin brown fringe dash
one second leap to safety
        sandstone rumble
           a mile downhill

What can I say?
must we continue
        comic opera heroes
        in a cowboy version
        of Hell?
You stomp out the gunpowder
in time
to free the lovely lady
3 inches from the sawblade
only to find ME
        tall black hat, twirled moustaches
tar & feathering your horse!

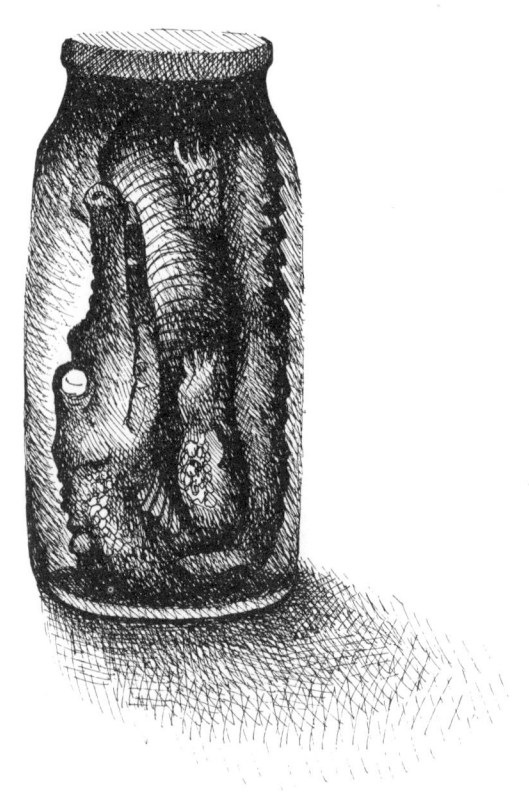

THE ATTIC

I wheezed & sneezed years
grade school nose-itch misery
   nights of ghost creaks
   foggy morning pees
   out open porthole window
   pinetrees

Flying squirrels loose in rock wool insulation
  an electrocuted alligator
  pickled in a jar
  his mate's head sewn up
  fake diamond eyes

I wrote poems here
U.S. Camera 1933 annual nudes
under my bed
   Scribbled late on saddleblanket
   hard wood floor
   a deer skull
   with steer horns
   over my head

One day woke & sprung
this cocoon silence
only to come back
to see the end

Tonight, my brother & I try the old porthole trick
missing badly, we both spatter the window frame,
sadly drunk on firey plums

Three Poems For Tommy

TOMMY

We camped a hundred
feet from the house
    chain-smoked King Sano
    filter kings
    inside our sleepingbags

backyard nightly frolick
with dogs
shoulder-strap sheath knives

    nothing on
    but jockstraps

then nothing at all

    "Give yourself ROOM
    to GROW!" you laughed

hopping over the doghouse

    big moon
    gone in the woods

Six Poems For Myself

THE RUBBER TREE THAT
LIVED TWENTY WINTERS

We buffed the leaves
with lemon oil
        clumsy indoor tree
        grew too big
our parakeets nibbled
the scarlet-pointed buds
           sharpened beaks
        on its alligator bark
I know why I adored
that tree—
the absurdity of it
splashing a cold northern parlor
green flipper leaves
        It took three men
        to carry it inside
        for the winter
We were surprised
when an early frost
in late fall nailed it
        I dreamed continually
        of all the rubber balls
           trapped inside
      those yellow
           tear drop leaves
flat dead on the patio floor

THE SNAKE NEST UNDER THE WILLOW TREE

Snakes slid out
the day they cut the big willow down
and we brought home
> handfuls
> black & yellow ribbons
> knots of fluttery tongued
> baby garters

All died or melted away
> eaten by cats
> pecked at by birds

generally forgotten
> by each of us
> after the willow wood
> stacked to dry
> went up a sooty chimney

along with the whippings
> climbings
> fallings

and the tiny snakes that curled
around your littlest finger

THE CURE

Uncle Raymond
had a hired man
took me up hayloft
by the ankle
& shook the breeze
out of me—
all I could see
was a mud-lot battlefield
of bristly hogs,
directly below

> "Now you listen good,
> boy, wet your bed
> once more & I'll fetch
> you up here
> & drop you for a sinker!"

that was the day
I shrank away from water,
no moisture touched my lips
that was the night
I wallowed in my dreams.
& pissed in the sky
like a scared piggy

UNCLE CHARLIE

25 boys in a leanto one night
played with eachother
by candlelight

Fat Uncle Charlie the scoutmaster
walked in at the final whack

    puffing his fat cigar

"Okay, that's it, all a youse
is goin home!"

    chewing his short cigar

"This is disgustin behavior
for a bunch of Boy Scouts!"

    munching his small cigar

"What would your mothers and fathers . . ."

   smack-chomp

"Youse guys really make me SICK!"

  gulp

THE GIRL IN THE WOODS:
FLASH BACK, NINETEEN FIFTY EIGHT

At last
I get her all alone
in the woods
on a blanket
completely disrobed
all glossy & fold-out lovely

What she doesn't know
is that I wore braces
all thru highschool
greaser hair, long on the sides
that horizontal sweep
collar up in back
spent hours detention hall
looking at my BAD feet
that couldn't jitterbug

I'm about to kiss her
I'm about to lie on top
of her & ██████ her

I spill bowls of potato chips
knock my bongos
from between my legs
upset somebody's coke
elbow somebody's chin
before I finally
quit goofing
  and get
    down
      to the
        business
          at
            hand

THE HIRED-HAND'S CORNFIELD GIFT

Just up from a nap
out in the yellowy tassles

The hired hand hung something loose
      back of my neck

Belly scale shiny feel

      A burnt umber
      copperhead necktie

THE DAYS OF YESTERYEAR

the bunk bed room
        holes in the wall
        where the plaster
        fell out
          were
        EYES
every contorted ceiling line
        a FACE

invisible panthers
        hungered
for my toes

the blue parakeet
        I took to bed with me
drowned in its own
        feathers

measles & pox
ate up my face
        & I seem to remember worrying
        that a certain part of me
        would fall off
        from under cover
        over use

MY BROTHER & THE BULL

   I bragged all day
   of animal conquests

   Huge droolsome beasts
     zonked
   by a fistful rose petals
    thistlepods
   plunked on the head

Meanwhile, my brother eight years old
    placed five fingers
   on the giant Angus bull's
    brass nose-ring
and lived to hear
   a chest-deep full-blown
    SNORT
   unexpected reply
    of very amiable disposition